A TASTE OF CHICKEN SOUP
FOR THE
CHRISTIAN SOUL

A TASTE OF CHICKEN SOUP FOR THE CHRISTIAN SOUL

Stories to Open the Hearts and Rekindle the Spirit

Jack Canfield
Mark Victor Hansen
Patty Aubery
Nancy Mitchell

Health Communications, Inc.
Deerfield Beach, Florida

www.hcibooks.com
www.chickensoup.com

Jewel. Reprinted by permission of Paul Della Valle. ©1994 Paul Della Valle. Taken from The Telegram & Gazette.

A Coincidence? Reprinted by permission of Ed Koper. ©1997 Ed Koper.

Safety Blanket. Reprinted by permission of Reverend Dr. Bruce Humphrey. ©1996 Reverend Dr. Bruce Humphrey.

Baptist Minister. Reprinted by permission of Lalia Winsett. ©1996 Lalia Winsett.

Faith. Reprinted by permission of Laverne W. Hall. ©1996 Laverne W. Hall.

Sunday School Lessons. Reprinted by permission of Susan Webber. ©1997 Susan Webber.

Wholly Holy Bloopers. Reprinted by permission of Richard Lederer. Excerpted from *Anguished English* by Richard Lederer. ©1987 Richard Lederer. First published by Wyrick and Company.

Shocking Generosity. Excerpted from Moments for Pastors by Sobert Strand. Reprinted by permission of New Leaf Press. ©1996 by New Leaf Press.

What Was in Jeremy's Egg? Reprinted by permission of Ida Mae Kempel. ©1988 Ida Mae Kempel.

Escalator Angel. Reprinted by permission of Richard Stanford. ©1996 Richard Stanford.

Erik's Old Man. Reprinted by permission of Nancy L. Dahlberg. ©1997 Nancy L. Dahlberg.

A Place Prepared by God. Reprinted by permission of Catherine E. Verlenden. ©1994 Catherine E. Verlenden.

A Tribute to Hawkins. Reprinted by permission of Rebecca Christian. ©1997 Rebecca Christian.

God's Own Son. Reprinted by permission of Kathleen Weber. ©1997 Kathleen Weber.

Library of Congress Cataloging-in-Publication Data is on file with the Library of Congress

ISBN 0-75730-511-3

Publisher: Health Communications, Inc.
3201 S.W. 15th Street
Deerfield Beach, FL 33442-8190

With love we dedicate this book to the millions of people who have read our previous books and to the 7,000 people who sent us stories, poems and quotes for possible inclusion in *Chicken Soup for the Christian Soul,* of which this is an excerpt. While we couldn't use everything you sent in, we were deeply touched by the heartfelt intention to share yourselves and your stories with us and our readers. Love to you!

"Finally, brethren, whatever things are true, whatever things are noble, whatever things are just, whatever things are pure, whatever things are lovely, whatever things are of good report, if there is any virtue and if there is anything praiseworthy—meditate on these things."

Philippians 4:8

Contents

Introduction

We feel truly blessed to have been able to create this book, which is just a "taste" of *Chicken Soup for the Christian Soul.* It has been a true labor of love for us, and like all divinely inspired projects, it has given us back much more than we have put into it. From the moment it was conceived, we have felt the power of love flowing through us and the divine hand of God directing us in our every step. Right from the beginning we have been experiencing miracles—from opening the Bible to just the right Scripture we needed, to finding the nephew of a writer we couldn't locate on the Internet! Our most fervent hope is that you will receive as much from reading this book as we did in compiling, editing and writing it.

We believe these stories will deepen

your Christian faith and expand your awareness of how to practice your Christian values in your day-to-day life. We hope they will open your heart, deepen your compassion and inspire you to greater acts of charity and philanthropy. And, perhaps most important, they will remind you that you are never alone, no matter how challenging your circumstances may be.

We pray that you experience the same love, inspiration, encouragement and comfort that these stories brought to us, and we ask that God may bless you!

Jewel

The IV's red light glowed in the early darkness, its beeping like a heartbeat, like the beat to Bette Midler's hit song about heroes, "Wind Beneath My Wings," that was playing softly from a radio in the nurses' station down the hall.

I had heard that popular song's lyrics dozens of times in my head over the weekend, late at night as I lay on a cot in the University of Massachusetts Medical Center and looked at my daughter Jewel.

Think it's strange for a 37-year-old man

to have a two-year-old girl as his hero? You don't know Jewel.

She's in remission now and odds are the leukemia will never come back. About 80 percent of the kids who get the most common childhood leukemia never relapse.

It's been a year full of hope—a year that brought a new baby daughter to our home—but it's been a rough year, too, a year punctuated by weekly trips to the clinic and a half dozen longer stays in the hospital. The first months of chemotherapy made all of Jewel's hair fall out. Some of the drugs made her hyper, some made her sleepy.

Through it all, there has been one constant—Jewel, who prays to "Baby Cheezits up in the sky" and who loves Babar cartoons and family hugs, has borne her illness with a heroic grace. I can't imagine any adult dealing with it as well. I know I haven't.

Jewel has been in the hospital for the last five days with an infection from the catheter in her chest. Her temperature rocketed from 98.6 degrees to 105 degrees in about five minutes when the bacteria in the catheter flushed into her blood. Jewel shook like a leaf as I screamed for a doctor. She, of course, handled it better than her old man and lay there saying, "I'm good, I'm good."

Last summer, Jewel battled the doctors and nurses who examined her. She was too young to understand why she had to be stuck with so many needles, she didn't understand her antagonists were actually angels of mercy striving to make her better. I will never forget the look in her eyes when I helped the nurses hold her for yet another blood test and she howled and her dark eyes screamed, "How can you, my protector, betray me?"

But she forgave me every time, kissing me with a loud smack—"moh"—and dancing when I played my harmonica. As the year went by, she gained an understanding about the extrinsic portions of her illness—the need for trips to the clinic, the catheter, the chemotherapy, the shots. The knowledge has made her wise beyond her years—and confident. What a talker she is. Sometimes she'll sit in the front window of our house, yelling at the top of her lungs to the older kids playing in the street.

"Beth, come play with me. Margy, come get me."

One day, I asked Dr. Newburger why so many children who get acute lymphoblastic leukemia survive when so many adults who get the same disease don't.

"Bottom line," he said, "we're not as tough."

Jewel's brother, Rocky, is nine. His summers should be all baseball and fishing and tree forts and Nintendo, not wondering about sickness and death.

About a month after Jewel was diagnosed with leukemia, Rocky and I were driving. Rocky was sitting in the front seat next to me, a bundle of skinny arms and legs in a Red Sox cap, looking at a purple sunset sky over a long, green field of corn.

I was telling him about the possibility of a bone marrow transplant. I was telling him that if it came down to it, he might be the perfect match for Jewel, how his bone marrow might save her life.

"Would it hurt?" he asked without looking away from the window.

"Yeah," I said.

"A lot?"

"It might hurt quite a bit."

"I don't want to hurt."

We drove on in silence, onto the highway.

"I'll do it," Rocky said suddenly, quietly. "I would die for my sister."

For the first time in a long time, I knew the tears welling up in my eyes weren't for sadness. And I knew, no matter what, leukemia was going to have one hell of a fight on its hands beating our family. There are too many little heroes in it.

Paul Della Valle

A Coincidence?

Give and it will be given to you; good measure, pressed down, shaken together, running over, they will pour into your lap. For whatever measure you deal out to others, it will be dealt to you in return.

LUKE 6:38 NIV

I was very proud of my daughter Emily. At only nine years old, she had been carefully saving her allowance money all year and trying to earn extra money by doing small jobs around the neighborhood. Emily was determined to save enough to buy a girl's mountain bike, an item for which she'd been longing, and she'd been faithfully putting her money away since the beginning of the year.

"How're you doing, honey?" I asked soon after Thanksgiving. I knew she had hoped to have all the money she needed by the end of the year.

"I have forty-nine dollars, Daddy," she said. "I'm not sure if I'm going to make it."

"You've worked so hard," I said encouragingly. "Keep it up. But you know that you can have your pick from my bicycle collection."

"Thanks, Daddy. But your bikes are so *old.*"

I smiled to myself because I knew she was right. As a collector of vintage bicycles, all my girls' bikes were 1950s models—not the kind a kid would choose today.

When the Christmas season arrived, Emily and I went comparison shopping, and she saw several less expensive bikes for which she thought she'd have to settle. As we left one store, she noticed a Salvation Army volunteer ringing his bell by a big kettle. "Can we give them something, Daddy?" she asked.

"Sorry, Em, I'm out of change," I replied.

Emily continued to work hard all through December, and it seemed she might make her goal after all. Then suddenly one day, she came downstairs to the kitchen and made an announcement to her mother.

"Mom," she said hesitantly, "you know all the money I've been saving?"

"Yes, dear," smiled my wife, Diane.

"God told me to give it to the poor people."

Diane knelt down to Emily's level. "That's a very kind thought, sweetheart. But you've been saving all year. Maybe you could give *some* of it."

Emily shook her head vigorously. "God said *all*."

When we saw she was serious, we gave her various suggestions about where she could contribute. But Emily had received specific instructions, and so one cold Sunday morning before Christmas, with little fanfare, she handed her total savings of $58 to a surprised and grateful Salvation Army volunteer.

Moved by Emily's selflessness, I suddenly noticed that a local car dealer was collecting used bicycles to refurbish and give to poor children for Christmas. And I realized that if my nine-year-old daughter could give away all her money, I could certainly give up one bike from my collection.

As I picked up a shiny but old-fashioned kid's bike from the line in the garage, it seemed as if a second bicycle in the line took on a glow. Should I give a *second* bike? No, certainly the one would be enough.

But as I got to my car, I couldn't shake the feeling that I should donate that second bike as well. And if Emily could follow heavenly instructions, I decided I could, too. I turned back and loaded the second bike into the trunk, then took off for the dealership.

When I delivered the bikes, the car dealer thanked me and said, "You're making two kids very happy, Mr. Koper. And here are your tickets."

"Tickets?" I asked.

"Yes. For each bike donated, we're giving away one chance to win a brand new men's 21-speed mountain bike from a local bike shop. So here are your tickets for two chances."

Why wasn't I surprised when that second ticket won the bike? "I can't believe you won!" laughed Diane, delighted.

"I didn't," I said. "It's pretty clear that Emily did."

And why wasn't I surprised when the bike dealer happily substituted a gorgeous new girl's mountain bike for the man's bike advertised?

Coincidence? Maybe. I like to think it was God's way of rewarding a little girl for a sacrifice beyond her years—while giving her dad a lesson in charity and the power of the Lord.

Ed Koper

Safety Blanket

When I was fresh out of the seminary, my wife, Kathy, and I moved with our two-year-old son, Nate, to a small native village in Alaska. The small three- and four-passenger planes we took on our connecting flights so terrified our little boy that he took his favorite blanket and covered his head until we set down on the small dirt landing strips. Later, during the long adjustment months that followed, when we were learning how to live in a new place among new people of a different culture, my son carried his security blanket everywhere, and it soon became soft and well-worn. He couldn't fall asleep until he had his blanket and could snuggle into its warmth.

The second year that we were in the village, I had a chance to guest speak at a mission conference in Seattle. While I was packing for the trip, my son followed me around the room, asking where I was going, and how long would I be gone, and why did I have to speak to those people, and was anyone going with me? Fine-tuning my speech in my mind, I was a little distracted and concerned about catching the small plane out of the village on time. My son seemed most worried about my having to fly out in bad weather on one of those small planes he feared so much. I reassured him that I would be fine, and I asked him to take care of his mom until I came back. With a hug at the door, I was off to the village landing strip and on to my speaking engagement.

When I got to the hotel in Seattle, I didn't have time to unpack until later that evening, and I was horrified when I opened my luggage and found my son's security blanket inside. I pictured my wife trying desperately to find the lost blanket as she prepared our son for bed. I immediately rushed to the phone to call Kathy and tell her that the blanket was in my luggage, so she could reassure our frantic son.

Kathy picked up the phone and barely had time to answer when I began to explain that the blanket was in my luggage and I had no idea how it had accidentally been packed. I was in the midst of my apology when Kathy calmed me down with the news that she already knew where the blanket was.

She told me that she had picked Nate up and held him by the window to let him watch me drive away from the house. She had suggested that they pray for "Daddy to have a safe trip." Knowing that our son would be most afraid of the small plane ride to the major airport, she prayed, "Dear Lord, please help Daddy feel safe on the little plane." When the prayer was over, our son Nate spoke up and comforted his mom. "Don't worry, Mom, I gave Daddy my blanket to keep him safe."

Reverend Dr. Bruce Humphrey

Baptist Minister

The heart has reasons
which reason cannot understand.

Blaise Pascal

I have a cousin who is a Baptist minister. When we were growing up, we only saw each other a couple of times a year. Now we see each other even less.

A few years ago, when I hadn't seen him for some time, I suddenly began thinking about him and his family. I just couldn't get them off my mind. And for some reason, I felt compelled to send him a check for $100. I thought about it for a few days and made more than one aborted trip to the post office. I finally mailed it with a letter saying I hope I wasn't offending him, but I believed the Lord wanted me to do this.

A couple of weeks later I received a reply. My cousin said it never ceased to amaze him how God worked in his life. And now God had once again shown him, through us, that he would always meet our needs. My cousin said the only concern he had was that I had sent too much. All he had needed was $97.56.

Lalia Winsett

Faith

Faith is to believe what we do not see,
and the reward of faith is to see
what we believe.

Saint Augustine

The fields were parched and brown from lack of rain, and the crops lay wilting from thirst. People were anxious and irritable as they searched the sky for any sign of relief. Days turned into arid weeks. No rain came.

The ministers of the local churches called for an hour of prayer on the town square the following Saturday. They requested that everyone bring an object of faith for inspiration.

At high noon on the appointed Saturday the townspeople turned out *en masse,* filling the square with anxious faces and hopeful hearts. The ministers were touched to see the variety of objects clutched in prayerful hands—holy books, crosses, rosaries.

When the hour ended, as if on magical command, a soft rain began to fall. Cheers swept the crowd as they held their treasured objects high in gratitude and praise. From the middle of the crowd one faith symbol seemed to overshadow all the others: A small nine-year-old child had brought an umbrella.

Laverne W. Hall

Sunday School Lessons

The Sunday school lesson for the day was about Noah's Ark, so the preschool teacher in our Kentucky church decided to get her small pupils involved by playing a game in which they identified animals.

"I'm going to describe something to you. Let's see if you can guess what it is. First: I'm furry with a bushy tail and I like to climb trees."

The children looked at her blankly.

"I also like to eat nuts, especially acorns."

No response. This wasn't going well at all!

"I'm usually brown or gray, but sometimes I can be black or red."

Desperate, the teacher turned to a perky four-year-old who was usually good about coming up with the answers. "Michelle, what do you think?"

Michelle looked hesitantly at her classmates and replied, "Well, I know the answer has to be Jesus—but it sure sounds like a squirrel to me!"

Susan Webber

Wholly Holy Bloopers

Humor is mankind's greatest blessing.

Mark Twain

The tradition of holy howlers popping up in religiously related documents continues undimmed.

Witness the following sampling of bona fide bloopers culled from various church bulletins and orders of service:

- The ladies of the church have cast off clothing of every kind, and they can be seen in the church basement Friday afternoon.

- On Sunday a special collection will be taken to defray the expense of the new carpet. All those wishing to do something on the carpet will please come forward to get a piece of paper.
- Irving Benson and Jessie Carter were married on Oct. 24 in the church. So ends a friendship that began in school days.
- This afternoon there will be a meeting in the south and north end of the church. Children will be baptized at both ends.
- For those of you who have children and don't know it, we have a nursery downstairs.
- The pastor will preach his farewell message, after which the choir will sing, "Break Forth into Joy."
- This being Easter Sunday, we will ask

Mrs. White to come forward and lay an egg on the altar.

- The choir will meet at the Larsen house for fun and sinning.
- Thursday at 5 p.m. there will be a meeting of the Little Mothers Club. All wishing to become little mothers will please meet with the minister in the study.
- During the absence of our pastor, we enjoyed the rare privilege of hearing a good sermon when J.F. Stubbs supplied our pulpit.
- Wednesday, the Ladies Literary Society will meet. Mrs. Clark will sing, "Put Me in My Little Bed," accompanied by the pastor.
- Next Sunday Mrs. Vinson will be soloist for the morning service. The pastor will then speak on "It's a Terrible Experience."
- Due to the Rector's illness, Wednesday's healing services will be discontinued

until further notice.

- Remember in prayer the many who are sick of our church and community.
- The eighth-graders will be presenting Shakespeare's Hamlet in the church basement on Friday at 7 P.M. The congregation is invited to attend this tragedy.
- Twenty-two members were present at the church meeting held at the home of Mrs. Marsha Crutchfield last evening. Mrs. Crutchfield and Mrs. Rankin sang a duet, "The Lord Knows Why."
- Smile at someone who is hard to love. Say "hell" to someone who doesn't care much about you.
- Today's Sermon:
  HOW MUCH CAN A MAN DRINK?
  with hymns from a full choir.
- Potluck supper: prayer and medication to follow.
- Don't let worry kill you off—let the church help.

Long may these bloopers live. Such unintentional levity brings lightness as well as light to many an otherwise dry church bulletin.

Richard Lederer
From Anguished English

Shocking Generosity

The story goes that while Robert Smith was taking his afternoon walk—part of his therapy in recovering from a massive heart attack—the phone rang and his wife, Delores, answered. The call was from the *Reader's Digest* Association Sweepstakes in New York. They were calling to inform the Smith Family that Robert had just won $1,500,000 and that in a few days the certified check would be arriving. Well, as you can imagine, Delores was absolutely ecstatic. Now all those dreams would come true!

But then she remembered her husband was just getting over his massive heart attack, and the doctor had said no excitement over anything. Delores was afraid that if she told him they had just won such a large sum, he would have another heart attack and die. What should she do? After some thought, she decided to call their pastor and ask his advice because he had had some experience in breaking difficult news to families.

Delores dialed. "Hello, Pastor Baldwin . . . this is Delores Smith."

The pastor replied, "Hi, Delores. How are you? And how is Bob?"

"I'm fine, thank you. And so is Bob. He's recovering nicely. But I've got a problem and I need your advice."

"Sure, if I can help, I'll be glad to," the pastor replied.

"Well, Pastor, I just got a call from the *Reader's Digest* Sweepstakes informing me that Bob has just won $1,500,000!"

"That's great!" said the pastor. "But what's the problem?"

"Well, I'm afraid that if I tell Bob, he'll get so excited that he will have another heart attack and drop dead. Can you help me?"

"Well, Delores, I think I can. Hold on, I'll be right over."

So in about an hour, Bob was back from his walk, and he and Delores and Pastor Baldwin were in the den having a nice chat. The pastor leaned toward Bob and said, "Bob, I've got a problem and need your advice."

"Sure, Pastor, if I can help, I'll be glad to," Bob said.

The pastor took a deep breath and went on, "It's a theoretical situation regarding Christian stewardship. What would a person—take you, for instance—do if all of a sudden you found out you had won $1,500,000? What would you do with all that money?"

"That's easy," Bob replied, "I'd start by giving $750,000 to the church."

Whereupon, Pastor Baldwin had a heart attack and dropped dead!

Excerpted from Moments for Pastors

What Was in Jeremy's Egg?

Jeremy was born with a twisted body, a slow mind and a chronic, terminal illness that had been slowly killing him all his young life. Still, his parents had tried to give him as normal a life as possible and had sent him to St. Theresa's Elementary School.

At the age of 12, Jeremy was only in second grade, seemingly unable to learn. His teacher, Doris Miller, often became exasperated with him. He would squirm in his seat, drool and make grunting noises.

At other times, he spoke clearly and distinctly, as if a spot of light had penetrated the darkness of his brain. Most of the time, however, Jeremy irritated his teacher. One day, she called his parents and asked them to come to St. Theresa's for a consultation.

As the Forresters sat quietly in the empty classroom, Doris said to them, "Jeremy really belongs in a special school. It isn't fair to him to be with younger children who don't have learning problems. Why, there is a five-year gap between his age and that of the other students!"

Mrs. Forrester cried softly into a tissue while her husband spoke. "Miss Miller," he said, "there is no school of that kind nearby. It would be a terrible shock for Jeremy if we had to take him out of this school. We know he really likes it here."

Doris sat for a long time after they left, staring at the snow outside the window. Its coldness seemed to seep into her soul. She wanted to sympathize with the

Forresters. After all, their only child had a terminal illness. But it wasn't fair to keep him in her class. She had 18 other youngsters to teach, and Jeremy was a distraction. Furthermore, he would never learn to read and write. Why waste any more time trying?

As she pondered the situation, guilt washed over her. "Oh God," she said aloud, "here I am complaining, when my problems are nothing compared with that poor family! Please help me to be more patient with Jeremy."

From that day on, she tried hard to ignore Jeremy's noises and his blank stares. Then one day he limped to her desk, dragging his bad leg behind him.

"I love you, Miss Miller," he exclaimed, loud enough for the whole class to hear. The other students snickered, and Doris's face turned red. She stammered, "Wh—why, that's very nice, Jeremy. Now please take your seat."

Spring came, and the children talked excitedly about the coming of Easter. Doris told them the story of Jesus, and then to emphasize the idea of new life springing forth, she gave each of the children a large plastic egg. "Now," she said to them, "I want you to take this home and bring it back tomorrow with something inside that shows new life. Do you understand?"

"Yes, Miss Miller!" the children responded enthusiastically—all except for Jeremy. He just listened intently; his eyes never left her face. He did not even make his usual noises.

Had he understood what she had said about Jesus's death and resurrection? Did he understand the assignment? Perhaps she should call his parents and explain the project to them.

That evening, Doris's kitchen sink stopped up. She called the landlord and waited an hour for him to come by and unclog it. After that, she still had to shop for groceries, iron a blouse and prepare a vocabulary test for the next day. She completely forgot about phoning Jeremy's parents.

The next morning, 19 children came to school, laughing and talking as they placed their eggs in the large wicker basket on Miss Miller's desk. After they completed their math lesson, it was time to open the eggs.

In the first egg, Doris found a flower. "Oh, yes, a flower is certainly a sign of new life," she said. "When plants peek through the ground, we know that spring is here." A small girl in the first row waved her arm. "That's my egg, Miss Miller," she called out.

The next egg contained a plastic butterfly, which looked very real. Doris held it up. "We all know that a caterpillar changes and grows into a beautiful butterfly. Yes, that is new life, too." Little Judy smiled proudly and said, "Miss Miller, that one is mine!"

Next, Doris found a rock with moss on it. She explained that moss, too, showed life. Billy spoke up from the back of the classroom. "My daddy helped me!" he beamed.

Then Doris opened the fourth egg. She gasped. The egg was empty! Surely it must be Jeremy's, she thought, and, of course, he did not understand her instructions. If only she had not forgotten to phone his parents. Because she did not want to embarrass him, she quietly set the egg aside and reached for another.

Suddenly Jeremy spoke up. "Miss Miller, aren't you going to talk about my egg?"

Flustered, Doris replied, "But Jeremy—your egg is empty!" He looked into her eyes and said softly, "Yes, but Jesus's tomb was empty, too!"

Time stopped. When she could speak again, Doris asked him, "Do you know why the tomb was empty?"

"Oh, yes!" Jeremy exclaimed. "Jesus was

killed and put in there. Then his Father raised him up!"

The recess bell rang. While the children excitedly ran out to the school yard, Doris cried. The cold inside her melted completely away.

Three months later, Jeremy died. Those who paid their respects at the mortuary were surprised to see 19 eggs on top of his casket, all of them empty.

Ida Mae Kempel

Escalator Angel

Live in such a way that those who know you but don't know God will come to know God because they know you.

Anonymous

The crisp February morning chilled the crowd that waited to catch the MARTA, Atlanta's public rail system. When the train arrived, I moved with the others toward vacant seats. Mechanical sounds punctuated the trip: the humming of electric motors and the loud bell before the doors slid shut.

As we settled into our parallel journeys, I looked around. I work at home, and consequently don't often take public transit at rush hour. This morning I was on my way into the city for a seminar. The size and diversity of the crowd on the train surprised me. In our single car, there were African-Americans, European-Americans and Asians—a generous representation of world society.

But there was no interaction. Business men and women had their briefcases open, poring over papers filled with charts and columns. Casually dressed students studied books. One young man had on headphones and swayed in a slow dance to his private music. I'm a fiction man, myself. I travel with a novel handy.

But today I didn't open it. I was too busy studying those around me; something felt strange.

I didn't realize what it was until I'd disembarked at Five Points, the connecting point for the east and west trains. In this cavernous space, I joined perhaps a thousand commuters waiting for their trains.

Here I realized what was so eerie: the total silence. One thousand people, packed cheek to jowl, looking straight ahead, pretending the others didn't exist. And I, a 50-year-old white man wearing a blue suit and glasses, was one of them. The only sound two stories under Atlanta's streets was the hum of the escalators.

And then came a woman's voice. "Good morning!"

The greeting echoed through the station. A thousand heads snapped up in unison, scanning the space. The voice had come from a woman riding the descending escalator on the far side of the platform. "How y'all this morning?"

She practically sang her words, punctuating her speech with long vowel extensions. People began to turn toward her.

The petite African-American woman

reached the bottom of the escalator and walked purposefully to the edge of the throng. She grabbed a surprised businessman's hand, shook it and looked him in the eye. "Good morning! How ya doing this morning?"

The man looked at the small woman who had him in her grip. He broke into a smile. "Fine, thank you."

Her clothes were a little ragged, but her purposeful smile overcame her stature and appearance as she moved through the crowd, shouting greetings, shaking hands and laughing freely. Finally, she looked across the tracks at the crowd on my side of the platform. "How ya'll folks over there this morning?

"Just fine!" I shouted back. Others answered with me. We surprised each other so much that we broke out laughing.

"That's good," she said. She paused and looked around. Now everyone was listening. "God sent me here to cheer you up this morning. And that's the God of the Jew, the Christian, the Muslim and any other religions ya'll brought or didn't bring along."

From where I stood, I could see a twinkle in her eye. Amazingly, the train station came alive with good-natured conversation. As we chatted with each other, few noticed the slight woman quietly ascend the up escalator.

When the northbound train arrived, I squeezed into a car already stuffed with riders. I didn't get much past the door and grabbed a chrome pole that already had hands of every racial color gripping it. My face looked straight into that of an African-American woman about my age. She wore a light yellow business suit. I sensed she didn't like the press of people around us.

Before I could stop myself, I said, "Good morning."

"What?" She seemed surprised.

"Good morning. How are you doing?" A few people watched us.

A smile overtook her. "Fine," she chuckled. "You know, nobody's asked me that this morning. Really, nobody ever says hello."

I grinned and told her about the unexpected visitor back at Five Points, wondering aloud if she might have been an angel. "Isn't that what angels do? They're messengers. That woman demonstrated the goodness of simply greeting each other, sharing our humanity, instead of guarding it."

Others around the pole joined the discussion, and smiles spread through the car.

The woman across from me, now grinning, said, "If it weren't so crowded in here, I'd give you a good hug. You've made my morning."

When the train arrived at my stop, I moved toward the door. "I hope you have a good day!" I called back to my fellow traveler.

"I will, and thank you."

As I looked back into the car, I saw lots

of smiles. People were chatting. Someone else touched my shoulder and waved good-bye. I felt happy and alive.

Since then, I've often wondered who that woman was. She didn't have wings; she ascended and descended an escalator and she spoke in a Southern drawl. But silent people who were temporarily buried two stories below Atlanta began to talk and laugh. A chilly February day felt warmer, and a shy guy like me suddenly hasn't been able to keep himself from greeting and talking with strangers on subway trains, elevators and airplanes. But isn't that what a more famous angelic message proclaimed: "Good will to all"?

In other words, good cheer is contagious. Pass it on.

Richard Stanford

Erik's Old Man

If you judge people, you have no time to love them.

Mother Teresa

Our family was driving from San Francisco to Los Angeles on Christmas Day. That year Christmas came on Sunday and we needed to be in Los Angeles on Monday morning, having spent Christmas Eve and Christmas morning with my husband's parents.

We stopped for lunch at a diner in King City. I was enjoying a review of the happiness and meanings of the day when my reverie was interrupted. I heard Erik, our one-year-old son, scream with glee in his high chair. "Hi there." (Two words he thought were one.) He pounded his fat baby hands—whack, whack—on the metal tray of the high chair. His face was alive with excitement, eyes wide, gums bared in a toothless grin. He wriggled and chirped and giggled, and then I saw the source of his merriment.

A tattered rag of a coat; greasy, worn. Baggy pants, both they and the zipper at half mast over a spindly body. Toes that poked out of would-be shoes. A shirt that had ring-around-the-collar all over and a face like none other. Gums as bare as Erik's. Hair unwashed, uncombed, unbearable. Whiskers too short for a beard but way beyond the shadow stage. And a nose so varicose that it looked like the map of New York. I was too far away to smell him, but I knew he smelled.

His hands were waving in the air,

flapping about on loose wrists. "Hi there, baby; hi there, big boy. I see ya, buster." Erik continued to laugh and call, "Hi there." Every call was answered. I shoved a cracker at Erik and he pulverized it in his tray. I turned the high chair. Erik screamed and twisted around to face his old buddy.

The waitresses' eyebrows were rising. Several diners went "ahem." This old geezer was creating a nuisance with my beautiful baby! Now the bum was shouting from across the room, "Do ya know peek-a-boo? Hey look, he knows peek-a-boo."

The old guy was drunk. Nobody thought anything was cute. My husband was embarrassed. I was humiliated. Even our six-year-old wanted to know why that man was talking so loud. We ate hurriedly and in silence, all except Erik, who continued to run through his repertoire with the bum.

My husband rose to pay the check, telling me to meet him in the parking lot. I grabbed Erik and headed for the exit. The old man sat poised and waiting, his chair directly between me and the door. *Lord, let me out of here before he speaks to me or Erik.*

I tried to side-step to put my back between Erik and any air the old man might be breathing. But Erik, with his eyes riveted on his best friend, leaned far over my arm, reaching out with both arms in a baby's pick-me-up gesture. In the split second of balancing my baby and turning to counter his weight, I came eye-to-eye with the old man. His eyes were imploring. "Would you let me hold your baby?"

There was no need to answer. Erik propelled himself from my arms into the man's and immediately laid his head on the man's ragged shoulder. The man's eyes closed and I saw tears hover beneath his lashes. His aged hands, full of grime and pain and hard labor, gently, so gently, cradled my baby's bottom and stroked his back.

The old man stroked and rocked Erik for a moment, then opened his eyes and looked squarely in mine. He said in a firm, commanding voice, "You take care of this baby."

I said, "I will."

He pried Erik from his chest, unwillingly, longingly, as though he were in pain. I held my arms open to receive my baby, and again the gentleman addressed me. "God bless you, ma'am. You've given me my Christmas present."

Nancy Dahlberg
Submitted by Walfred Erickson

Prayer Is the Key

A missionary was serving as a medic at a small field hospital in Africa. Periodically he had to travel by bicycle through the jungle to a nearby city for supplies. It was a two-day trip so he had to camp out overnight. He had made this trip several times without incident. One day, however, he arrived at his destination and saw two men fighting. One was seriously hurt, so he treated him and witnessed to him and went about his business.

Upon arriving in the city again several

weeks later, he was approached by the man he had treated earlier. "I know you carry money and medicine," said the man to the missionary. "Some friends and I followed you into the jungle the night you treated me, knowing you would camp overnight. We waited for you to go to sleep and planned to kill you and take your money and drugs. Just as we started moving into the campsite, we saw you were surrounded by 26 armed guards. There were only six of us and we knew then we couldn't possibly get near you, so we left."

Hearing this the missionary laughed and said," That's impossible. I can assure you I was alone in the campsite."

The young man pressed his point: "No sir, I was not the only one to see the guards. My friends also saw them, and we all counted them. We were frightened. It was because of those guards that we left you alone."

Several months later, the missionary

attended a church presentation in Michigan where he told about his experiences in Africa. One of the congregants jumped to his feet, interrupting the missionary, and said something that left everyone in the church stunned.

"We were there with you in spirit," said the man. The missionary looked perplexed. The man continued. "On that night in Africa, it was morning here. I stopped at the church to gather some materials for an out-of-town trip to another parish. But as I put my bags into the trunk, I felt the Lord leading me to pray for you. The urging was so great I called the men in the church together to pray for you."

Then the man turned around and said, "Will all of those men who met with the Lord that morning please stand?" One by one they stood—all 26 of them!

Anonymous
Submitted by Murray Moerman

A Place Prepared by God

The Lord will watch over your coming and going both now and forevermore.

PSALM 121:8 NIV

The green ceramic tiles of the bathroom floor cooled my baked-out skin. I sat back against the wall, my legs drawn up, clutching my Bible, folding into myself. And I wondered where this fear had come from, consuming enough to send me into the bathroom of a strange motel, hiding my torment from my sleeping sons in the next room.

Until then, I'd been doing pretty well.

We'd made it through a sad divorce, and somehow God had given me the strength to move my young sons across the country, to a new house, a new job, a new life. I'd felt capable and even excited.

But now, in the middle of the night, in the middle of nowhere, I saw myself for what I truly was: alone. And in danger.

The danger was not amorphous. It had a name: the Mojave Desert. And it was just outside the door.

So far we'd driven three days across the South, through sweltering July heat. My little car and I both had miles and experience under our fan belts, but we were still chugging along. Yet the trip, which had started so hopefully, had now turned sour. Perhaps it was the monotony of days of endless driving. During this last day, particularly, all the fears that had dogged me during the past difficult months found long stretches of thinking time to spend with me in the car.

As we neared the Mojave Desert, our final hurdle to our arrival in California, I realized the danger we faced and how vulnerable I was.

I'd heard every horror story—radiators that boil dry, blow-outs, relentless sun that crisps fragile flesh, the sheer isolation of the long asphalt strip that winds its way through the rocky desolation. Hours with no bathroom, no water . . . nothing. No help.

That frightened me the most. If we got into trouble, who would help us? How could I protect my children if the worst happened? They were dependent on me, and for the first time in my life, I had . . . nobody.

I lived it all ahead of time, there on the bathroom floor of our motel room.

This is ridiculous! I told myself. *You've got to get to sleep! Your only hope is to be up at five, crossing as much of the Mojave as possible before the arrival of the punishing sun. Pull yourself together. Get a grip!*

But I couldn't. I felt as if all the desert demons were after me.

Noticing the Bible clutched in my hand, I realized I hadn't had time for that day's devotional. Almost mechanically, I opened it to my bookmark, skimming for the verses where I'd left off somewhere in Revelation. *Let's see . . . chapter 12.* I began to read. *Oh, yes, the woman and the dragon.* A familiar passage. A scene of dramatic rescue as the child was snatched up to God and to his throne.

I read on: "The woman fled into the desert to a place prepared for her by God, where she might be taken care of . . ."

I sat up straight, my heart pounding. *The woman fled into the desert to a place prepared for her by God.*

In a very real sense, I was a woman in flight myself. Looking for a safe place, fleeing into the desert. The words were alive for me, as if I were hearing, not reading them.

Could it be that I wasn't alone? That my Heavenly Father was already out there, in that frightening landscape, preparing a place for me?

In a twinkling the desert was no longer a sinister threat to our safety but a haven to be embraced. The fear in my throat dissipated slowly as I sat there, eyes closed, beside the toilet, embracing my open Bible.

In a short while, I, too, had settled for the night and was fast asleep.

My nerves were steady when the alarm went off. I got the kids up, fixed breakfast from the cooler and loaded up. It would be a long day, 16 hours behind the wheel. I was grateful for the reassurance I'd received the night before. It didn't feel as immediate this morning. But I wanted to believe that the desert was somewhere that I might "be taken care of." I took a deep breath, and off we went.

We drove in the dark for a cool hour. Then the sun rose, full throttle. Not a cloud to be seen. Or another car, for that matter. I looked at the dash, checking dials and gauges one more time. Temperature was holding okay, but my palms were getting a little sweaty.

I laid the back of my hand against the windshield. Hot already! *"Thank you, Lord, for the air conditioning! Please, keep our little car going. Please take care of us.* ". . . a place prepared for her by God, where she might be taken care of . . ." I turned the words over again in my heart.

Almost subconsciously at first, I became aware that a shadow had fallen over the car. No matter the bends and curves in the road, the shadow bent and curved with us. The sky was perfectly blue and clear, except for this one little cloud whose shadow tracked our vehicle like a homing device.

After a couple of hours, we stopped at the one gasoline oasis in that vast expanse. I could see the cloud, like a patient friend, waiting for us at the highway. We resumed our journey, and the shadow cocooned us once more. Under its protection we traveled for another two hours. I relaxed. I laughed out loud with delight at the one who was taking care of me.

As the highway tunneled us back into civilization, our cloud became one of many. It disappeared without me even being aware of it. But its presence remained with me, from that day to this. For I know that I dwell in a place prepared for me, so that I may be taken care of. And I am no longer afraid.

Catherine E. Verlenden

A Tribute to Hawkins

When my husband called to announce that his new promotion was going to take us away from a lovely, unglaciated pocket of northeast Iowa, my first instinct was the "right" one.

"Congratulations. I'm proud of you," I chirped like a brave little wife in a 1930s movie. My second, more honest instinct, was to wail, "What will we do without Hawkins?"

Any working mother who has ever moved can tell you that the worst chore of moving is not unpacking the jar of bacon drippings that movers have ever-so-delicately wrapped and put in the same box as the silk lamp shades. Nor is it finding a new hairdresser clever enough to camouflage the knobs on the back of her head so she doesn't look like a kingfisher bird.

The worst task by far is searching for the perfect baby-sitter. Any mother worthy of her title approaches it with her stomach queasy from fear and guilt.

When Kate was four years old and Nicholas almost a year, I decided to take them to a baby-sitter a couple of days a week so I could concentrate on getting my career off the ground. I felt a little silly calling a retired drama coach I had just met the week before; after all, I barely knew her, and she had been out of the childrearing scene for decades. But Helen seemed so savvy and well-connected that I just knew she'd give me a good lead.

"I think I might know someone," she mused, indulging in the flair for mystery that must have served her well as a theatrical director, "but I can't tell you who it is until I talk to her."

Helen called back in a few days to tell me that hersister-in-law, Evelyn Hawkins, a retired farm widow who had recently moved into an apartment in town, had experience from rearing scads of kids and grandbabies, smarts, and the patience of Job.

What first struck me on meeting this trim, soft-spoken woman was her extraordinary calmness. Though she seemed a little restrained and serious until I knew her well, I could tell right away that behind her reserve was a great deal of substance.

A wooden cross hanging in her kitchen and a sampler in her upstairs hall gave me clues about her deep faith. The sampler, neatly cross-stitched in green on white, showed a window with a curtain blowing in a gentle breeze. The maxim underneath was, "When God closes a door, he opens a window."

Yet Hawkins was so private and humble that it was months before I learned by accident that the daily "walk" she was returning from when we arrived, however brutal the weather, was really a trip to church.

Though she never told the kids what to call her, she came to be known as Hawkins because Evelyn somehow didn't sound respectful enough to me, and Mrs. Hawkins was too big a mouthful for my little ones to handle. Though the kids are too diplomatic to say so, I am sure that Hawkins' steady style of child rearing was a welcome relief from my own rock-swat-hug-holler-kiss method. The worst of it is, I don't even believe in swatting and hollering.

Though she was an outwardly conservative person who reared her children in a less permissive era than this one, Hawkins was really more of a free spirit than I am. While she was teaching my children, I was learning from her too.

When Kate went through her jealous stage and pretended to be a baby, she wouldn't buy my song and dance about the glories of being a 'big girl.' Later, I learned that Hawkins simply let her drink milk from a baby bottle until she got so tired of the slow flow that she begged for a glass. And when Nick insisted he was a dog one day, he got to eat his Cheerios hunkered down over a plastic bowl set on the floor.

The first time we asked if the kids could spend the night at her house, I warned Hawkins that Nick was going through a stage of waking up frightened, and that she might have to lie with him a few minutes to get him back to sleep. When we arrived in the morning, still a little apprehensive about how it had gone, the kids crowed, "We had a slumber party. We slept in Hawkins' bed!"

Hawkins told us mildly, "Oh well, I figured we might as well start the night all in the same bed." I could just picture the three of them in the upstairs bedroom, Hawkins in her high necked gown with one of my children asleep in the crook of each arm.

Another thing I learned from Hawkins' example was that life is made up of small tasks so we might as well take pleasure in them when we can. Whether it was carefully arranging a circle of gumdrops on a Swedish tea ring my children "helped" her bake or mending the ripped seat of her bachelor brother's pants with careful, even stitches, Hawkins did things right. She went about the small businesses of life so cheerfully that her efforts did not so much demean her as ennoble the tasks. The garment she entered in the county fair came back with a judge's accolade that made her eyes glow—"the finest workmanship."

She took care of my children with the same unhurried grace. She had a way of solemnly inclining her head toward a child who was embroidering a long-winded tale. It put me to shame, because in the same situation, my eyes glaze over; I murmur, "ummm . . .," and I think my own thoughts. Her attitude made me feel that the checks we gave her were secondary to the pleasure she took in filling our need, so much so that the moment of paying her was awkward.

It was little wonder that after two years of taking my children to her, leaving Hawkins was one of the hardest parts of leaving Decorah. I knew I was not likely to find another sitter who embodied the best qualities of Mary Poppins and Captain Kangaroo. Only *her* eyes were dry when she pressed a four-leaf clover charm into the palm of Kate's hand. "Remember," she whispered to my sobbing daughter, "when God closes a door, he opens a window."

Rebecca Christian

God's Own Son

As Mary rocks her baby boy
She's filled with sadness, filled with joy
She looks upon that tiny face
And sees the hope of every race.

Her heart is filled with a mother's glow
And she never wants to let him go.
She'll see him run and laugh and play
And longs to keep him safe each day.

His life won't be an easy one,
His destiny hard, as God's own Son.

Mary sees the miracles he'll perform,
The lepers healed and free from scorn.
The lame will walk, the blind will see.
She sees his love will set us free.

And then she sees him on a cross.
She feels his pain and feels our loss.
She knows his life must come to this.
She sheds a tear and gives a kiss.

His life won't be an easy one,
His destiny hard, as God's own Son.

So as Christmastime draws near
And we are all so "busy" here,
With shopping, baking, trees of green
Let's ask, what does this really mean?

Let's take a moment from the fuss,
And think of all their gifts to us:
A mother's love, a baby boy,
Peace and comfort, love and joy.

For he was born for everyone,
His destiny, God's only Son.

Kathleen Weber

More Chicken Soup?

Many of the stories and poems you have read in this book were submitted by readers like you who had read earlier *Chicken Soup for the Soul* books. We publish at least five or six *Chicken Soup for the Soul* books every year. We invite you to contribute a story to one of these future volumes.

Stories may be up to 1,200 words and must uplift or inspire. You may submit an original piece or something you clip out of the local newspaper, a magazine, a church bulletin or a company newsletter. It could also be your favorite quotation you've put on your refrigerator door or a personal experience that has touched you deeply.

To obtain a copy of our submission guidelines and a listing of upcoming *Chicken Soup* books, please write, fax or check one of our Web sites.

Chicken Soup for the Soul
P.O. Box 30880, Santa Barbara, CA 93130
Fax: 805-563-2945
To e-mail or visit our Web sites:
www.chickensoup.com

Passing It On!

It is a tradition to donate a portion of the net profits of every original Chicken Soup for the Soul book to several charities related to the theme of the book. Proceeds from sales of the original Chicken Soup for the Christian Soul is donated to the following charities:

Feed The Children

This is an international, nonprofit Christian organization providing food, clothing, medical equipment and other necessities to people who lack these essentials because of famine, drought, flood, war or other calamities all over the world. Feed The Children was formed by Larry Jones in 1979 and has distributed over 280 million pounds of relief commodities. Today, Feed the Children programs supplement 123,000 meals per day.

Feed the Children, P.O. Box 36, Oklahoma City, OK 73101-0036.

Habitat for Humanity

An international organization, Habitat for Humanity works with people around the world, from all walks of life, building houses and developing communities in partnership with those in need. Habitat for Humanity helps meet the universal necessity for a safe, decent place to live. This basic need is what compels Habitat to improve the human condition; and in so doing, build God's kingdom on Earth, one house, one family at a time.

HFHI, 121 Habitat Street, Americus, GA 31709-3498.

Covenant House

Covenant House is the largest privately-funded childcare agency in the U.S. serving over 400,000 youth in the last 25 years. It was incorporated in New York City in 1972 and has since expanded to New Orleans, Houston, Fort Lauderdale, Orlando, Los Angeles, Anchorage, Newark, Atlantic City and Washington, D.C. It has also established programs in Guatemala, Honduras, Mexico and Toronto, Canada.

They provide residential and non-residential services (food, shelter, clothing, crisis care, health care, education, vocational preparation, drug abuse treatment, prevention programs, legal services, recreation, mother/child programs, transitional living programs) to more than 44,000 homeless and runaway youth. Their Covenant House Nineline (1-800-999-9999) received almost 88,000 crisis calls from youngsters all over the country who needed immediate help and had nowhere else to turn.

Covenant House, 346 W. 17th Street, New York, NY 10011.

Who Is Jack Canfield?

Jack Canfield is one of America's leading experts in the development of human potential and personal effectiveness. He is both a dynamic, entertaining speaker and a highly sought-after trainer. Jack has a wonderful ability to inform and inspire audiences toward increased levels of self-esteem and peak performance.

In addition to the *Chicken Soup for the Soul* series, Jack has coauthored numerous books, including his most recent release, *The Success Principles, How to Get From Where*

You Are to Where You Want to Be with Janet Switzer, *The Aladdin Factor* with Mark Victor Hansen, *100 Ways to Build Self-Concept in the Classroom* with Harold C. Wells, *Heart at Work* with Jacqueline Miller and *The Power of Focus* with Les Hewitt and Mark Victor Hansen.

Jack is regularly seen on television shows such as *Good Morning America, 20/20* and *NBC Nightly News.* For further information about Jack's books, tapes and training programs, or to schedule him for a presentation, please contact:

Self-Esteem Seminars
P.O. Box 30880
Santa Barbara, CA 93130
Phone: 805-563-2935 • Fax: 805-563-2945
Web site: *www.chickensoup.com*

Who Is Mark Victor Hansen?

In the area of human potential, no one is better known and more respected than Mark Victor Hansen. For more than thirty years, Mark has focused solely on helping people from all walks of life reshape their personal vision of what's possible. .

He is a sought-after keynote speaker, bestselling author and marketing maven. Mark is a prolific writer with many best-selling books such as *The One Minute Millionaire, The Power of Focus, The Aladdin Factor* and *Dare to Win,* in addition to the

Chicken Soup for the Soul series.

Mark has appeared on *Oprah, CNN* and *The Today Show,* and has been featured in *Time, U.S. News & World Report, USA Today, New York Times* and *Entrepreneur* and countless radio and newspaper interviews.

As a passionate philanthropist and humanitarian, he has been the recipient of numerous awards that honor his entrepreneurial spirit, philanthropic heart and business acumen for his extraordinary life achievements, which stand as a powerful example that the free enterprise system still offers opportunity to all.

Mark Victor Hansen & Associates, Inc.
P.O. Box 7665
Newport Beach, CA 92658
Phone: 949-764-2640 • Fax: 949-722-6912
Web site: *www.markvictorhansen.com*

Who Is Patty Aubery?

Patty Aubery is the vice president of The Canfield Training Group and Self-Esteem Seminars, Inc. Patty came to work for Jack Canfield in 1989, when Jack still ran his organization out of his house. Patty has been working with Jack since the birth of *Chicken Soup for the Soul* and can remember the days of struggling to market the book. Patty says, "I can remember sitting at flea markets in 100 degree weather trying to sell the book and people would stop, look and walk to the next booth! . . . Now

14 million copies have been sold of the first 11 books." Patty is the coauthor of *Chicken Soup for the Surviving Soul: 101 Stories of Courage and Inspiration from Those Who Have Survived Cancer.* Patty can be reached at The Canfield Training Group, P. O. Box 30880, Santa Barbara, CA 93130, or by calling 1-800-237-8336, or faxing 805-563-2945.

Who Is Nancy Mitchell?

Nancy Mitchell is the director of publishing for The Canfield Group and manager of all copyrights and permissions. She graduated from Arizona State University in May of 1994 with a B.S. in Nursing. After graduation Nancy worked at Good Samaritan Regional Medical Center in Phoenix, Arizona, in the Cardiovascular Intensive Care Unit. Four months later Nancy moved town to Los Angeles, where sister and coauthor, Patty Aubery, offered her a part-time job working for Jack

Canfield and Mark Victor Hansen. Nancy's intentions were to help finish *A 2nd Helping of Chicken Soup for the Soul* and then return to nursing. However, in December of that year, she was asked to continue on full time at The Canfield Group. Nancy put nursing on hold and became the director of publishing, working closely with Jack and Mark on all *Chicken Soup for the Soul* projects.

Nancy can be reached at The Canfield Group, P. O. Box 30880, Santa Barbara, CA 93130, or by calling 1-800-237-8336, or faxing 805-563-2945, or via e-mail at *www.chickensoup.com.*

Contributors

If you would like to contact any of the contributors for information about their writing or would like to invite them to speak in your community, look for their contact information included in their biography.

Rebecca Christian is a playright, travel writer, speaker and columnist raised in Dubuque, Iowa. Her work has appeared in over 100 magazines and newspapers. She can be reached at 641 Alta Vista St., Dubuque, IA 52001, or by calling 319-582-9193.

Reverend Nancy Dahlberg is currently serving the United Church of Christ as an Interim Minister. She continues to write, speak and lead seminars on topics which motivate and inspire Christian service and leadership. Write to her at P.O. Box 3100, York, PA 17402.

Laverne W. Hall has done major radio, TV and newspaper interviews and has published one book of poetry. She can be reached at 3994 Menlo Dr., Atlanta, GA 30340, or by calling 770-491-8887.

Rev. Dr. Bruce Humphrey pastors Trinity Presbyterian Church, which has grown from 250 to 650 members during his 10 years of leadership. The author of five books, Bruce is known as a storyteller-preacher. With two earned doctorates, Bruce speaks at seminars, camps, retreats and renewals. He can be reached at 630 Park Ave., Prescott, AZ 86303.

Ida Mae Kempel has been widely published in Christian magazines. She is also the author of three books. The latest, *What Was in Jeremy's Egg? and Other Stories,* is a compilation of some of her work. To order books or to request an interview, write to Nascent Press, 2137 Otis Dr. #302, Alameda, CA 94501, or call 510-523-8741.

Edward Koper is not an internationally recognized speaker, but is a happily married man with a wonderful wife, Diane, and two terrific daughters named Emily and Rachel. Ed feels fortunate to have had his life touched by God in a small way and hopes everyone learns to recognize God's hand in their lives. Ed can be reached at 908-566-3130.

Richard Lederer has published more than two thousand articles and books about language, including his blooper series *Anguished English, More Anguished English* and *Fractured English.* He has been elected International Punster of the Year and profiled in *The New Yorker* and *People* magazine. His weekly column, Looking at Language, appears in newspapers and magazines throughout the United States. He makes 150 speaking appearances each year and is a regular language commentator for public radio. He can be reached by mail at 9974 Scripps Ranch Blvd., Ste. 201, San Diego, CA 92131, by calling 619-549-6788 or via e-mail at *richard.lederer@pobox.com;//www.pobox.com/~verbivore.*

Richard Stanford is a Presbyterian minister and recently became a full-time writer. He has had several articles and stories published. He currently has a novel and two short stories under consideration for publication. You can write to Richard at 1219 Mohican Trail, Stone Mountain, GA 30083, or e-mail to *Richard_Stanford@msn.com.*

Catherine Verlenden is a lay counselor, short-term missionary and freelance writer of articles for Christian publications.

Kathleen Weber and her husband have raised five children in Boston, New York. She is a Catholic school librarian and also works at Weight Watchers. Kathy is active in many church and community organizations and enjoys poetry as well as the arts.